Overcoming Depression Through Positive Thinking

("Harness the Power of Positive Thinking to Break Free from Depression and Reclaim Your Life")

Written By
Jasmine Brown

Introduction

Overview of Depression

Depression is more than just feeling down or going through a rough patch. It's a serious mental health condition that can affect every aspect of your life, from how you think and feel to how you manage daily activities. Many who suffer from depression experience persistent sadness, loss of interest in things they once enjoyed, fatigue, difficulty concentrating, and changes in appetite or sleep patterns. It can be triggered by life events, such as the loss of a loved one, trauma, or even genetic predisposition. Depression is not a weakness; it's a medical condition that requires understanding, care, and effective coping mechanisms.

Importance of Positive Thinking in Mental Health

Positive thinking plays a crucial role in overcoming depression. While it's not a magic cure, it can significantly reshape how you respond to life's challenges. When caught in the depths of depression, negative thoughts often dominate, leading to a cycle of despair, self-doubt, and helplessness. Positive thinking doesn't mean ignoring problems or pretending everything is fine—it's about shifting your mental outlook. By learning to recognize and challenge negative thoughts and replacing them with constructive, realistic, and optimistic ones, you can begin to foster hope, resilience, and self-compassion.

The power of positive thinking lies in its ability to change your brain's patterns. With practice, it helps to rewire the brain for positivity, making it easier to cope with stress, anxiety, and the struggles that depression often brings.

A Personal Story to Illustrate the Journey

Let me introduce you to Emma. For years, Emma struggled with depression after losing her job unexpectedly. At first, it was manageable, but over time, she found herself withdrawing from friends, losing interest in her favorite hobbies, and feeling overwhelmed by feelings of worthlessness. She would wake up every morning with dread, convinced that nothing would get better.

After months of battling depression, Emma sought help. One key turning point in her recovery came when her therapist introduced her to the concept of positive thinking. It seemed impossible at first—how could she think positively when everything felt so bleak? But Emma began small: writing one positive thought each day, recognizing when negative thoughts dominated her mind, and slowly challenging them with alternative, hopeful perspectives. Over time, her mindset shifted, and she found herself feeling lighter, more empowered, and able to navigate life's challenges with newfound resilience. Emma's story isn't unique, and like her, anyone struggling with depression can learn to harness the power of positive thinking to reclaim their life.

What Readers Can Expect from This Book

This book is designed as a step-by-step guide to help you break free from the grip of depression using positive thinking techniques. In the chapters that follow, you will:

- Gain a deeper understanding of what depression is and how it impacts your thought processes.

☐ Learn to identify and challenge the negative thoughts that keep you trapped in a cycle of despair.
☐ Develop practical strategies to cultivate positive thinking, such as gratitude, affirmations, mindfulness, and self-care.
☐ Explore how to build supportive relationships and manage setbacks with grace and resilience.
☐ Hear from others who have walked a similar path and found healing through positive thinking.

Whether you're at the beginning of your recovery journey or seeking tools to sustain your progress, this book offers actionable advice and encouragement to help you transform your mindset and take back control of your mental well-being.

Chapter 1: Understanding Depression

What is Depression? Common Symptoms and Triggers

Depression, medically known as major depressive disorder, is a mental health condition characterized by prolonged feelings of sadness, hopelessness, and a lack of interest in daily activities. It goes far beyond normal mood fluctuations and can deeply affect a person's emotional, cognitive, and physical well-being. Depression interferes with the ability to function in everyday life, making it difficult to work, socialize, or enjoy activities that once brought joy.

Some of the most common symptoms of depression include:

- Persistent feelings of sadness or emptiness.
- Loss of interest in activities once enjoyed.
- Fatigue or lack of energy.
- Difficulty concentrating or making decisions.

- ☐ Changes in appetite or weight (eating too much or too little).
- ☐ Sleep disturbances (insomnia or excessive sleeping).
- ☐ Feelings of worthlessness or excessive guilt.
- ☐ Irritability or restlessness.
- ☐ Thoughts of death or suicide.

Triggers for depression vary from person to person. For some, it can be situational, triggered by a major life event such as losing a loved one, financial hardship, or a significant change in one's life circumstances. For others, it may develop without a clear reason, stemming from genetic predisposition, chemical imbalances in the brain, or underlying medical conditions.

Differentiating Between Sadness and Clinical Depression

Everyone experiences sadness or moments of feeling down, but depression is much more than temporary sadness. It's important to understand the distinction between sadness and clinical depression to know when help is needed.

Sadness is a normal emotion that is often triggered by life events. It tends to be short-lived and usually fades as situations change or improve. People experiencing sadness can still find moments of pleasure or relief, and their feelings don't typically disrupt their ability to carry out daily responsibilities.

Depression, on the other hand, is pervasive. It lingers for weeks, months, or even years, affecting how you think, feel, and behave. It can lead to a loss of interest in nearly all activities, even those that were once enjoyable. Depression often comes with physical symptoms such as fatigue, body aches, and sleep disturbances. While sadness typically improves with time or positive life changes, depression may not go away on its own and often requires treatment or intervention.

The Role of Negative Thinking in Depression

One of the most significant contributors to depression is the cycle of negative thinking. People struggling with depression often experience what is known as **automatic negative thoughts (ANTs)**. These thoughts are typically self-critical, pessimistic, and catastrophic, and they often arise without conscious control.

Examples of automatic negative thoughts include:
- "I'm worthless."
- "Nothing will ever get better."
- "Everyone else is doing fine, and I'm a failure."
- "Why even bother trying?"

This constant stream of negativity reinforces feelings of hopelessness and helplessness, making it difficult to break free from the depression cycle. It also impacts self-esteem, leading individuals to believe they are incapable of change or undeserving of happiness. Over time, negative thinking can become deeply ingrained, creating a distorted view of reality.

However, it's important to note that negative thinking patterns can be challenged and changed. By becoming aware of these destructive thoughts and replacing them with more realistic, balanced perspectives, individuals can begin to alleviate the mental burden of depression.

The Science of Depression: How the Brain and Mind are Affected

Depression isn't just a mental condition it has a profound effect on the brain. Advances in neuroscience have shown that depression is linked to changes in the structure and function of various brain regions. Understanding how depression affects the brain can offer insight into why it's such a difficult condition to overcome and why certain treatments, such as medication and therapy, are effective.

1. Imbalance of Neurotransmitters

The brain relies on neurotransmitters—chemical messengers—to regulate mood, emotions, and behavior. In people with depression, certain neurotransmitters, such as serotonin, dopamine, and norepinephrine, may be imbalanced. These chemicals play a critical role in promoting feelings of happiness, motivation, and reward. When they are deficient or not functioning properly, it can lead to feelings of sadness, fatigue, and apathy.

2. The Role of the Amygdala

The amygdala is the part of the brain responsible for processing emotions, particularly fear and negative emotions. In people with depression, the amygdala tends to be overactive, making them more sensitive to negative stimuli. This heightened activity can make it difficult to manage stress and can exacerbate feelings of anxiety and sadness.

3. The Prefrontal Cortex

The prefrontal cortex is involved in decision-making, regulating emotions, and reasoning. Depression has been shown to reduce activity in this area of the brain, which may explain why individuals with depression often struggle to make decisions, concentrate, or regulate their emotions effectively.

4. The Hippocampus and Memory

The hippocampus is critical for memory formation and emotional regulation. Studies have found that people with depression often have a smaller hippocampus, likely due to the high levels of stress that accompany the disorder. Chronic stress can cause the hippocampus to shrink, leading to memory problems and an inability to process emotions in a healthy way.

5. Cortisol and Stress

Cortisol, the body's stress hormone, is typically elevated in individuals with depression. This prolonged exposure to high levels of cortisol can damage the brain over time, contributing to the shrinkage of the hippocampus and impairing emotional regulation. The constant presence of cortisol also puts the body in a state of heightened stress, leading to physical symptoms such as fatigue, headaches, and muscle tension.

Conclusion: Understanding Depression and Its Impact

Depression is a complex condition that affects both the mind and body. It involves more than just a low mood—it impacts how you think, how your brain functions, and even how you physically feel. While it can feel overwhelming, understanding the nature of depression is the first step toward managing and overcoming it.

In the chapters to follow, we'll delve deeper into how you can challenge the negative thinking patterns that feed depression, cultivate healthier habits, and start the journey toward healing using positive thinking techniques

Chapter 2: The Power of Thoughts

Introduction to Cognitive Behavioral Therapy (CBT) Principles

Cognitive Behavioral Therapy (CBT) is one of the most effective tools used to combat depression. The core idea behind CBT is that our thoughts, emotions, and behaviors are interconnected. Negative thoughts can lead to negative emotions and behaviors, which in turn reinforce the negative thought patterns, creating a self-perpetuating cycle. CBT teaches us how to recognize these unhelpful patterns and replace them with healthier, more balanced thinking.

In essence, CBT works by:
- **Identifying** problematic thoughts that contribute to feelings of depression.
- **Challenging** these thoughts by questioning their accuracy and relevance.
- **Replacing** negative, distorted thoughts with positive, realistic alternatives.

CBT empowers individuals to take control of their mental state by altering the way they think about and respond to their experiences. It's a process of rewiring your thinking, allowing for more adaptive, hopeful, and productive thought patterns.

How Thoughts Influence Emotions and Behavior

The way we think directly affects how we feel and how we act. Negative thoughts, such as "I'll never succeed" or "No one cares about me," create negative emotions like sadness, hopelessness, and fear. These emotions often lead to behaviors that can worsen depression, such as avoiding social activities, isolating yourself, or neglecting responsibilities.

For example:
- Thought: "I always fail at everything I try."
- Emotion: Feeling hopeless, worthless, or defeated.
- Behavior: Avoiding new challenges, not applying for jobs, or giving up on personal goals.

Over time, these behaviors reinforce the initial negative thought, solidifying the belief that you're incapable of change. It becomes a vicious cycle.

By learning to recognize and challenge negative thoughts, you can break this cycle. Instead of responding with automatic negative thinking, CBT encourages you to consider alternative perspectives:

- Thought: "I didn't do as well as I hoped this time, but I've succeeded before, and I can improve."
- Emotion: A sense of determination and motivation.
- Behavior: Trying again, seeking help, or making adjustments to improve.

This shift in thinking leads to healthier emotional responses and more constructive actions, fostering personal growth and well-being.

Recognizing Negative Thought Patterns

To break the cycle of negative thinking, the first step is to identify the common patterns that distort reality. These thought patterns are often automatic and deeply ingrained, but they can be unlearned with practice. Here are some common negative thought patterns, often referred to as **cognitive distortions**, that contribute to depression:

1. Catastrophizing

- **What it is:** Believing that the worst possible outcome will occur or exaggerating the severity of a situation.
- **Example:** "I failed this test, so I'm going to fail the entire course and ruin my future."
- **How to challenge it:** Ask yourself, "What's the worst that can really happen? Is this outcome likely?" Consider more realistic outcomes, such as being able to retake the test or seek help.

2. Black-and-White Thinking (All-or-Nothing Thinking)

- **What it is:** Viewing situations in extremes, without considering any middle ground.
- **Example:** "If I'm not perfect, I'm a total failure."
- **How to challenge it:** Recognize that life is rarely all or nothing. Most situations fall in a gray area, and small mistakes don't define your worth.

3. Overgeneralization

- **What it is:** Drawing broad conclusions based on a single event or experience.
- **Example:** "I didn't get the job I wanted; nothing ever goes right for me."

☐ **How to challenge it:** Focus on the specifics of the situation rather than making sweeping generalizations. Remind yourself of past successes.

4. Emotional Reasoning

☐ **What it is:** Assuming that your negative feelings reflect the truth about a situation.

☐ **Example:** "I feel like a failure, so I must be one."

☐ **How to challenge it:** Understand that feelings are not facts. Just because you feel a certain way doesn't mean it's objectively true.

5. Personalization

☐ **What it is:** Blaming yourself for events beyond your control or assuming undue responsibility for negative outcomes.

☐ **Example:** "My friend didn't call me back because I must have upset her."

☐ **How to challenge it:** Look at the evidence and consider other possible reasons. Ask yourself, "Is this really about me, or could there be another explanation?"

By becoming aware of these distorted thought patterns, you can start to challenge and correct them, opening the door to healthier, more realistic thinking.

How Positive Thinking Can Rewire the Brain

The brain is incredibly adaptable, and one of its most remarkable traits is neuroplasticity—the ability to change and reorganize itself by forming new neural connections. Depression often creates well-worn pathways in the brain, where negative thinking becomes the default setting. However, through the practice of positive thinking, you can literally rewire your brain.

Positive thinking exercises help create new neural pathways that reinforce optimism, hope, and resilience. The more you practice positive thinking, the stronger these pathways become, making it easier to naturally gravitate toward positive thoughts over time.

Here's how positive thinking can impact the brain:

1. **Strengthening Neural Pathways**
    * When you focus on positive thoughts, you activate certain areas of the brain associated with

feelings of happiness and well-being, such as the prefrontal cortex. Repeated activation of these areas helps strengthen the neural connections, making positive thinking more automatic.

2. Reducing the Impact of Stress

☐ Positive thinking reduces the brain's stress response. When you approach situations with optimism or a solution-oriented mindset, the brain produces fewer stress hormones like cortisol, which can exacerbate depression. This can lower anxiety levels and improve emotional regulation.

3. Boosting Neurotransmitters

☐ Positive thinking can increase levels of neurotransmitters like dopamine and serotonin—chemicals that play key roles in regulating mood and feelings of pleasure. By focusing on positive thoughts, you promote the release of these "feel-good" chemicals, helping to counteract the chemical imbalances often associated with depression.

4. Enhancing Problem-Solving and Creativity

☐ Studies show that positive thinking broadens the brain's sense of possibilities, allowing you to think more creatively and solve problems more effectively. When your brain is stuck in negative thinking, it tends to narrow its focus to threats or worst-case scenarios. Positive thinking, on the other hand, encourages flexibility and openness, leading to better decision-making.

By practicing techniques like gratitude, affirmations, and reframing negative thoughts, you can gradually reprogram your brain for positivity. This doesn't mean ignoring challenges or difficulties, but rather approaching them from a place of empowerment and optimism. Over time, you'll find it easier to manage depression and cultivate a mindset that supports mental and emotional well-being.

Conclusion

Your thoughts have incredible power over your emotions and behavior, and understanding the principles behind Cognitive Behavioral Therapy (CBT) is key to overcoming depression. By recognizing negative thought patterns and replacing them with more constructive, positive ones, you can start to shift your mindset and create a more hopeful, resilient outlook on life. With practice, positive thinking can reshape your brain and help you build a mental framework that supports long-term recovery from depression.

Chapter 3: Identifying and Challenging Negative Thoughts

Learning to Recognize Automatic Negative Thoughts (ANTs)

One of the most significant contributors to depression is the prevalence of **Automatic Negative Thoughts (ANTs)** those quick, pessimistic thoughts that seem to pop up out of nowhere. These thoughts often go unnoticed because they are automatic, deeply ingrained in your thinking patterns. They distort your perception of yourself, others, and the world around you, feeding into feelings of helplessness, worthlessness, and despair.

Examples of common ANTs include:
- [ ] "I'm not good enough."
- [ ] "I always mess things up."
- [ ] "No one cares about me."
- [ ] "I'll never be happy again."

Recognizing these thoughts is the first step to overcoming them. ANTs often sound like an internal voice criticizing your abilities, undermining your self-worth, or predicting worst-case scenarios. They tend to surface in moments of stress, self-doubt, or fear and often seem convincing, despite being based on distorted perceptions of reality.

To start identifying ANTs, practice paying attention to your thoughts, especially in moments of heightened emotion. Ask yourself:
- "What was I thinking when I started feeling upset?"
- "Is there a particular situation that triggers these thoughts?"

By becoming aware of these automatic thoughts, you can begin the process of challenging and reframing them, rather than letting them dictate your emotions and actions.

The Impact of Self-Talk on Mental Health

Self-talk is the inner dialogue you have with yourself. It shapes your beliefs, influences your behavior, and impacts your mental health. When self-talk is predominantly negative, it can reinforce the thought patterns that contribute to depression. Over time, negative self-talk can become habitual, creating a vicious cycle of self-doubt, pessimism, and low self-esteem.

Negative self-talk often manifests in different ways, such as:

- ☐ **Self-criticism:** "I'm so stupid. I can't do anything right."
- ☐ **Pessimism:** "This is never going to work out."
- ☐ **Perfectionism:** "If it's not perfect, it's a failure."

These patterns of thinking erode confidence and make it harder to believe that change is possible. On the flip side, positive self-talk can have the opposite effect. Encouraging, supportive self-talk can foster resilience, boost self-esteem, and help you navigate challenges with greater ease.

To improve your self-talk, start by noticing when you're being overly critical or pessimistic. Then, consciously replace those negative statements with more compassionate, realistic, and constructive ones. For example:

- ☐ **Negative self-talk:** "I failed at this, so I must be a failure."
- ☐ **Positive self-talk:** "I didn't do well this time, but I can learn from this and try again."

The goal is to be kind to yourself, just as you would be to a friend facing the same challenges. Positive self-talk doesn't mean ignoring reality; it's about framing situations in a way that encourages growth, not defeat.

Techniques for Challenging and Reframing Negative Thoughts

Once you've identified your ANTs and recognized the impact of negative self-talk, the next step is to **challenge and reframe** these thoughts. This involves questioning the accuracy of your negative thoughts and finding more balanced, realistic alternatives. Here are some practical techniques for doing this:

1. **Question the Evidence**
   - When a negative thought arises, ask yourself, "What evidence do I have to support this thought?" and "What evidence do I have that contradicts this thought?"
   - **Example:** "I always fail" → Evidence might show that you've succeeded in many things before, even if this one instance didn't go as planned.

2. **Consider Alternative Explanations**

- ☐ Ask yourself if there could be another explanation for the situation. This helps prevent you from jumping to negative conclusions.

- ☐ **Example:** "My friend didn't reply to my message because she's mad at me" → An alternative explanation might be that she's busy or didn't see the message.

3. **Think in Shades of Gray**

- ☐ Avoid black-and-white thinking. Instead, see situations on a spectrum, recognizing that there's often a middle ground.

- ☐ **Example:** "I'm either a total success or a complete failure" → Reframe it as, "I'm doing my best, and I'm learning as I go."

4. **Use Positive Affirmations**

- ☐ Replace negative thoughts with positive affirmations—statements that promote self-belief and resilience.

- ☐ **Example:** "I'm not capable of doing this" → Replace it with, "I'm learning, and I'll get better with practice."

5. Practice Self-Compassion
- ☐ Be gentle with yourself. Recognize that making mistakes is part of being human, and it's okay to not have everything figured out.
- ☐ **Example:** "I messed up again" → Reframe it as, "Everyone makes mistakes. What can I learn from this?"

By actively challenging your negative thoughts and replacing them with healthier alternatives, you begin to weaken the hold that ANTs have on your mind. Over time, this process will become more automatic, allowing you to approach difficult situations with greater confidence and positivity.

Exercises: Journaling and Tracking Thoughts

One of the most effective ways to identify, challenge, and reframe negative thoughts is through journaling and tracking your thoughts. These exercises help you become more aware of your mental patterns and give you a space to practice reframing them in a constructive way.

1. Journaling

- Set aside time each day to write down your thoughts and feelings. Journaling helps you process emotions and brings clarity to your internal experiences. It's also a great way to track your progress as you work on challenging negative thoughts.
- **Prompt ideas:**
- "What negative thoughts have I had today? Are they based on facts or assumptions?"
- "What evidence do I have for and against these thoughts?"
- "How can I reframe these thoughts to be more positive or realistic?"

2. Thought Record Exercise

- This CBT technique involves breaking down your thought process into steps and analyzing it. Use a simple table to track:
- **Situation:** Describe the situation that triggered the negative thought.
- **Negative Thought:** Write down the specific thought that arose.

- ☐ **Emotion:** Note the emotion(s) you felt (e.g., sadness, anxiety).
- ☐ **Evidence:** Consider the evidence for and against this thought.
- ☐ **Alternative Thought:** Reframe the negative thought with a more balanced and realistic one.
- ☐ **Outcome:** Note how this alternative thought made you feel.

Example:
- ☐ **Situation:** I made a mistake at work.
- ☐ **Negative Thought:** "I'm terrible at my job."
- ☐ **Emotion:** Embarrassment, frustration.
- ☐ **Evidence For:** "I made a mistake."
- ☐ **Evidence Against:** "I've done well on other tasks, and mistakes are a part of learning."
- ☐ **Alternative Thought:** "I made a mistake, but I can learn from it and improve."
- ☐ **Outcome:** Relief, determination.

3. Tracking Progress

Over time, tracking your thoughts will help you see patterns and recognize which areas need more attention. You'll also begin to notice a shift in your mindset as you regularly practice reframing negative thoughts.

Conclusion

Identifying and challenging negative thoughts is a crucial step in breaking free from the cycle of depression. By learning to recognize Automatic Negative Thoughts (ANTs) and the impact of self-talk on your mental health, you can begin to reshape your thinking patterns. With techniques like questioning evidence, using alternative explanations, and practicing self-compassion, you can reframe negative thoughts and replace them with healthier, more empowering ones. Journaling and tracking your thoughts offer practical tools to monitor your progress and solidify these new ways of thinking, leading to a more positive and resilient mindset.

Chapter 4: Building a Positive Mindset

Shifting Perspective: From Victim to Empowerment

One of the most significant shifts in overcoming depression is moving from a victim mindset to an empowered one. When you feel trapped by depression, it's easy to view yourself as a victim of circumstances, powerless to change your situation. This mindset feeds feelings of helplessness and reinforces negative thought patterns. However, by reframing your perspective, you can begin to take control of your narrative and empower yourself to make positive changes.

The key is recognizing that while you may not be able to control everything that happens in your life, you **can** control how you respond. Instead of focusing on what's going wrong or what you can't change, shift your attention to what you can do. This doesn't mean dismissing your struggles but acknowledging your ability to respond with resilience.

- **Victim mindset:** "Nothing ever goes right for me. I'm stuck in this situation."
- **Empowered mindset:** "This situation is challenging, but I have the power to make changes, however small, and take steps toward a better future."

To cultivate an empowered mindset, start by acknowledging the areas of your life where you do have control. Focus on setting small, achievable goals, and celebrate your progress. Remember, empowerment comes from within—it's not about avoiding challenges but about facing them with the confidence that you can rise above them.

Practicing Gratitude: The Science and Benefits

Gratitude is one of the simplest yet most powerful tools for building a positive mindset. Scientific research has shown that practicing gratitude can lead to a host of mental health benefits, including improved mood, increased resilience, and reduced symptoms of depression. When you focus on what you're grateful for, you shift your attention away from what's lacking or going wrong in your life and instead emphasize the positive aspects.

The practice of gratitude can rewire your brain over time. It enhances the production of dopamine and serotonin, neurotransmitters responsible for feelings of happiness and well-being. Additionally, gratitude helps to reduce stress and anxiety by grounding you in the present moment and fostering a sense of contentment.

Ways to practice gratitude include:
- **Gratitude Journals:** Each day, write down three things you're grateful for. These can be as simple as having a warm cup of tea or a kind word from a friend. Over time, this habit will help you focus more on the positive aspects of your life.
- **Gratitude Meditation:** Spend a few minutes each day meditating on the things you're thankful for,

allowing yourself to fully experience feelings of appreciation.

☐ **Expressing Gratitude:** Tell the people in your life that you're grateful for them. Whether it's through a note, a message, or a conversation, expressing gratitude strengthens relationships and boosts your own sense of well-being.

The more you practice gratitude, the more you'll notice positive things in your life, no matter how small, helping to shift your mindset toward one of abundance rather than scarcity.

Focusing on Strengths, Not Weaknesses

Depression often makes it easy to focus on your shortcomings or what you perceive as weaknesses. This self-critical mindset can make you feel inadequate or unworthy, feeding into negative thought patterns. However, every person has strengths—unique talents, abilities, and qualities that they can draw upon, especially in challenging times.

Building a positive mindset involves shifting your focus from your weaknesses to your strengths. Here are some strategies to help:

1. **Identify Your Strengths:** Make a list of your strengths, even if they seem small or insignificant. Consider your personal qualities (e.g., kindness, resilience), skills (e.g., problem-solving, creativity), and accomplishments (e.g., finishing a project, helping a friend).

2. **Leverage Your Strengths:** Once you've identified your strengths, think about how you can use them to overcome challenges or achieve your goals. If you're struggling with a problem, ask yourself, "How can I use my creativity or persistence to solve this?"

3. **Celebrate Your Wins:** Instead of fixating on what you didn't do or areas where you fell short, celebrate your accomplishments. Recognize your efforts and progress, no matter how small.

4. **Reframe Weaknesses:** Everyone has areas where they're not as strong, and that's okay. Instead of viewing these as personal failings, see them as opportunities for growth or collaboration. A weakness in one area doesn't diminish your overall worth or capabilities.

When you focus on your strengths, you boost your self-confidence and cultivate a mindset that emphasizes possibility, rather than limitation.

Affirmations and Visualizations for Positive Reinforcement

Affirmations are positive statements that reinforce your belief in yourself and your abilities. They are designed to counter negative self-talk and create new, positive thought patterns. When practiced regularly, affirmations can help reprogram your subconscious mind to focus on positive outcomes.

Here's how to create and use affirmations effectively:
1. **Keep Them Positive:** Affirmations should be phrased in the positive. Instead of saying, "I am not a failure," say, "I am capable and resilient."

2. **Make Them Present Tense:** State your affirmations as if they are already true. For example, "I am confident in my abilities," even if you're still working on building that confidence.

3. **Personalize Your Affirmations:** Use affirmations that resonate with you and address the specific areas of your life where you want to create positive change.

4. **Visualize Success:** Pair your affirmations with visualization. Picture yourself achieving your goals, feeling confident, and thriving. Visualization helps solidify these

positive images in your mind, making them feel more real and attainable.

Some example affirmations might include:
- "I am worthy of love and happiness."
- "I trust myself to handle challenges with grace."
- "I am growing stronger and more capable every day."

Exercises: Daily Affirmations and Gratitude Journals

Daily Affirmations
- **Morning Routine:** Start your day with 3-5 positive affirmations. Stand in front of the mirror, say them out loud, and look yourself in the eye. Repeat them with conviction, allowing yourself to truly believe the words.

- **Throughout the Day:** When you catch yourself engaging in negative self-talk, replace those thoughts with your affirmations. For example, if you think, "I can't handle this," shift to, "I am strong enough to get through this."

Gratitude Journals
- **End-of-Day Practice:** Every night before bed, write down three things you're grateful for. These can

range from major events (e.g., a promotion at work) to small, everyday joys (e.g., a sunny afternoon, a pleasant conversation). This practice helps shift your focus to the positive aspects of your day.

☐ **Weekly Reflection:** At the end of each week, look back at your gratitude journal and reflect on the things you've been thankful for. Notice any patterns that emerge, and take pride in the positive aspects of your life.

Conclusion

Building a positive mindset is a journey that requires consistent practice and intention. By shifting your perspective from victimhood to empowerment, practicing gratitude, focusing on your strengths, and using affirmations and visualizations, you can reshape the way you view yourself and the world around you. Through daily exercises like affirmations and gratitude journaling, you'll develop habits that reinforce positivity, resilience, and self-belief, helping you move forward with confidence in your ability to overcome depression and lead a fulfilling life.

Chapter 5: Managing Stress and Anxiety

The Connection Between Depression, Stress, and Anxiety

Stress and anxiety often go hand-in-hand with depression, creating a vicious cycle that can make it difficult to break free from negative emotions. Stress arises when we feel overwhelmed by the demands placed on us—whether from work, relationships, or personal pressures. Anxiety is the fear or worry about things that may happen in the future. Together, these can contribute to feelings of hopelessness and exacerbate depression.

When stress is chronic, it keeps your mind and body in a constant state of tension, leading to burnout, exhaustion, and a sense of being "on edge." Anxiety feeds into this by heightening your fear response, often resulting in panic, racing thoughts, and difficulty concentrating. Left unchecked, stress and anxiety can fuel depressive thoughts and make it even harder to cope with daily life.

Managing stress and anxiety effectively is essential for reducing their impact on depression. By learning strategies to calm the mind and manage the body's stress response, you can regain control over your mental and emotional well-being.

Mindfulness and Meditation: Calming the Mind

Mindfulness and meditation are powerful tools for managing stress and anxiety. These practices help bring your attention to the present moment, breaking the cycle of worry about the future or rumination over the past two habits that often worsen anxiety and depression.

- [ ] **Mindfulness** involves paying attention to your thoughts, feelings, and surroundings in a non-judgmental way. When you're mindful, you observe your thoughts without getting caught up in them, allowing you to respond more calmly to stressful situations.

For example, if you notice feelings of anxiety rising, instead of reacting with panic or avoidance, mindfulness encourages you to acknowledge the feeling and gently bring your focus back to the present. This practice reduces the power that anxious thoughts have over you.

☐ **Meditation** is a more structured form of mindfulness, where you dedicate time each day to focus your mind, often on your breath or a mantra. Regular meditation practice has been shown to reduce anxiety, lower stress levels, and improve overall emotional regulation. Even a few minutes of meditation each day can help build resilience to stress.

Steps for a Basic Mindfulness Meditation:
1. Find a quiet space where you won't be disturbed.
2. Sit comfortably, with your back straight and your hands resting on your lap.
3. Close your eyes and bring your attention to your breath. Notice the sensation of the air moving in and out of your body.

4. When your mind starts to wander (which it will), gently bring your focus back to your breath. Don't judge yourself for getting distracted—this is part of the process.
5. Continue this for 5-10 minutes, or longer if you feel comfortable.

Over time, mindfulness and meditation help to calm the mind, reduce the intensity of anxious thoughts, and foster a sense of peace and control.

Breathing Techniques to Reduce Anxiety

When you're stressed or anxious, your body's fight-or-flight response kicks in, causing shallow, rapid breathing, increased heart rate, and tension. Learning to control your breathing is one of the quickest and most effective ways to calm your nervous system and reduce anxiety.

Here are a few breathing techniques to practice when you're feeling anxious:

1. **Deep Belly Breathing** (Diaphragmatic Breathing):
   - Sit or lie down in a comfortable position. Place one hand on your chest and the other on your abdomen.
   - Inhale deeply through your nose, allowing your belly (not your chest) to rise as you fill your lungs with air.

□ Exhale slowly through your mouth, letting your belly fall.

□ Repeat for 5-10 breaths, focusing on the rise and fall of your abdomen.

This technique encourages deep, slow breathing, which activates the body's relaxation response and helps reduce feelings of anxiety.

2. **4-7-8 Breathing:**

□ Inhale through your nose for a count of 4.

□ Hold your breath for a count of 7.

□ Exhale through your mouth for a count of 8.

□ Repeat this cycle 4-5 times.

The 4-7-8 technique helps slow your breathing, giving your body time to relax and your mind time to refocus.

3. **Box Breathing** (Square Breathing):

□ Inhale through your nose for 4 counts.

□ Hold your breath for 4 counts.

□ Exhale through your mouth for 4 counts.

□ Hold your breath for 4 counts again.

□ Repeat this cycle for 1-2 minutes.

Box breathing helps regulate your breath and provides a calming effect by balancing oxygen levels in the body.

Finding Balance: Learning to Say No and Setting Boundaries

One major contributor to stress and anxiety is overcommitting or failing to set healthy boundaries. When you constantly say "yes" to others, whether at work, with friends, or in your family you risk becoming overwhelmed, which leads to burnout. Learning to say "no" and setting clear boundaries is crucial for protecting your mental health.

1. **Recognize Your Limits:** Understand that you have physical, emotional, and mental limits. Acknowledge when you're reaching these limits and take steps to protect your well-being by setting boundaries.

2. **Learn to Say No:** Saying "no" is not selfish; it's necessary for self-care. When you feel overburdened, practice politely declining additional responsibilities or requests. For example, you could say, "I appreciate the offer, but I need to focus on my current commitments."

3. **Communicate Boundaries Clearly:** Whether in personal relationships or work settings, be clear about your boundaries. If you're not comfortable with certain demands, express your concerns respectfully and assertively. For instance, if you need quiet time after work

to recharge, let your family know so they can support your needs.

4. **Balance Time and Energy:** Set priorities for how you spend your time and energy. Recognize that it's okay to take breaks and recharge when needed. This balance is key to avoiding stress-related burnout and maintaining a healthy, positive mindset.

Setting boundaries helps reduce the pressure and expectations that lead to chronic stress, allowing you to manage anxiety more effectively.

Exercises: Breathing and Relaxation Techniques

Breathing Exercises for Daily Practice
- **Morning Routine:** Begin your day with 5 minutes of deep belly breathing or 4-7-8 breathing. This will help set a calm, focused tone for the day.
- **During Stressful Moments:** Whenever you feel stress or anxiety creeping in, take a 2-minute break to practice box breathing. This can be done at work, home, or anywhere else you need to center yourself.

Relaxation Techniques

- **Progressive Muscle Relaxation:** Lie down in a comfortable position. Starting from your toes, tense each muscle group in your body for 5 seconds, then release. Move up through your legs, torso, arms, and finally your face. This technique helps release tension and calm the nervous system.

- **Guided Meditation for Stress Relief:** Use a guided meditation app or video to practice stress-relieving meditation. These can be especially helpful when you're feeling overwhelmed and need assistance focusing.

Conclusion

Managing stress and anxiety is an essential part of overcoming depression and fostering a positive mindset. By understanding the connection between these states and learning techniques such as mindfulness, meditation, and controlled breathing, you can bring calm and balance back into your life. Setting healthy boundaries and knowing when to say no are also key strategies for protecting your mental and emotional well-being. Regularly practicing breathing exercises and relaxation techniques will give you the tools you need to face life's challenges with a clearer mind and a more peaceful heart.

Chapter 6: Creating Healthy Habits

Building Positive Habits That Boost Mental Health

Healthy habits form the foundation of good mental health, providing structure, stability, and positive reinforcement in your daily life. When battling depression, it's easy to fall into negative routines—such as isolation, poor sleep patterns, or avoiding responsibilities. These behaviors often reinforce the cycle of depression, making it harder to break free. However, cultivating small, positive habits can have a profound impact on your emotional well-being and gradually help you overcome feelings of hopelessness and low motivation.

Positive habits act as building blocks for a healthier mind and body. They instill a sense of accomplishment, no matter how small, and help you regain control over your life. The key is to start small, with manageable goals, and gradually build on your success. Habits such as regular physical activity, proper nutrition, and consistent sleep patterns can significantly improve your mood and energy levels over time.

- ☐ **Start Small:** Instead of trying to overhaul your life all at once, begin by implementing one small positive habit. For example, you could aim to drink more water each day or take a 10-minute walk outside.
- ☐ **Be Consistent:** Habits thrive on consistency. Try to perform your new habit at the same time each day, which will help it become a natural part of your routine.
- ☐ **Track Your Progress:** Use a habit tracker or journal to monitor your progress. Celebrate your wins, even if they feel minor. This positive reinforcement will encourage you to keep going.

The Role of Physical Activity and Diet in Mental Well-being

Physical activity and a balanced diet are essential components of mental health. When your body is well-nourished and physically active, it helps regulate mood, reduce stress, and improve cognitive function.

1. Physical Activity:

- Regular exercise is one of the most effective natural treatments for depression. Physical activity boosts the production of endorphins, the brain's "feel-good" chemicals, which help alleviate stress and elevate mood. It also reduces inflammation, improves sleep, and increases energy levels—all of which contribute to better mental health.

You don't need to engage in intense workouts to see the benefits. Even moderate exercise, such as walking, yoga, or cycling, can have a significant impact on your mood and well-being.

Exercise Ideas:

- ☐ Start with 15-30 minutes of activity a day, such as walking or stretching.
- ☐ Consider activities that you enjoy, such as dancing, swimming, or group sports.
- ☐ Gradually increase the intensity or duration as you become more comfortable.

2. **Diet:**

- ☐ Nutrition plays a critical role in maintaining mental health. A diet rich in whole foods, fruits, vegetables, lean proteins, and healthy fats can help support brain function, stabilize mood, and reduce inflammation. Conversely, a diet high in processed foods, sugars, and unhealthy fats can contribute to mood swings, fatigue, and increased anxiety.

Key Nutrients for Mental Health:

- ☐ **Omega-3 Fatty Acids:** Found in fish like salmon and walnuts, omega-3s support brain health and reduce symptoms of depression.
- ☐ **B Vitamins:** These vitamins, found in leafy greens, beans, and whole grains, help regulate mood by supporting neurotransmitter function.
- ☐ **Antioxidants:** Found in fruits and vegetables, antioxidants protect the brain from oxidative stress and inflammation.

Eating a balanced diet can help you feel more energized, focused, and emotionally balanced. Additionally, drinking plenty of water and reducing caffeine and alcohol intake will further support your mental and physical well-being.

The Power of Routine and Structure in Overcoming Depression

Depression often leads to feelings of chaos or lack of control over life. Creating a daily routine helps bring structure and stability, which is essential for managing depression. A consistent routine can provide a sense of purpose and predictability, reducing feelings of overwhelm and helping you stay grounded.

When you have a routine, your brain becomes more efficient at managing tasks, which reduces decision fatigue and conserves mental energy. For people with depression, even simple tasks can feel daunting, so building a daily structure around regular activities can help you manage your day more effectively.

- ☐ **Morning Routines:** Start your day with a consistent morning routine that includes habits like getting out of bed at the same time, showering, eating breakfast, and engaging in a brief activity like journaling or stretching. This sets a positive tone for the day.
- ☐ **Break Tasks into Smaller Steps:** For larger tasks, break them into smaller, manageable steps. Completing even a small portion of a task can give you a sense of accomplishment and motivation to continue.
- ☐ **Evening Wind-Down:** Create an evening routine that helps you relax and prepare for a restful night's sleep. This could include reading, meditating, or doing a brief reflection on the day.

Breaking the Cycle of Rumination

One of the challenges of depression is the tendency to ruminate—replaying negative thoughts or events over and over in your mind. Rumination exacerbates feelings of helplessness, anxiety, and sadness, making it difficult to escape the cycle of negative thinking. However, by creating healthy habits that distract your mind and shift your focus, you can break free from this destructive pattern.

- ☐ **Practice Mindfulness:** Mindfulness exercises, such as meditation or deep breathing, help you focus on the present moment rather than dwelling on past events or future worries. This practice can reduce the hold that rumination has on your mind.

- ☐ **Engage in Creative Activities:** Hobbies such as painting, writing, or gardening can redirect your mind away from negative thoughts. Creative activities stimulate different parts of the brain and help you express emotions in a healthy, constructive way.

- ☐ **Physical Movement:** Physical activity is a powerful tool for interrupting rumination. When you're physically engaged, your mind is less likely to spiral into negative thinking. Even taking a brief walk or stretching can help refocus your thoughts.

Exercises: Habit Formation and Tracking Progress

Habit Formation
- ☐ **The 21/90 Rule:** It's often said that it takes 21 days to form a habit and 90 days to make it a lifestyle.

Start by committing to a new habit for 21 days. Whether it's a morning walk, journaling, or eating a healthy breakfast, focus on consistency.

☐ **Anchor Habits:** Link a new habit to an existing routine. For example, if you want to start meditating, do it right after brushing your teeth in the morning. This helps create a natural connection between the two activities, making the new habit easier to adopt.

Habit Tracking:
Use a habit tracker or journal to monitor your progress. Each day, check off the habits you've completed. This visual reminder will keep you accountable and help you see your progress over time. You can track simple habits such as:
- Exercising for 30 minutes.
- Drinking 8 glasses of water.
- Writing in a gratitude journal.

By tracking your habits, you can identify patterns and make adjustments when needed. Over time, this practice will reinforce positive behaviors and give you a sense of accomplishment.

Conclusion

Creating healthy habits is a crucial part of overcoming depression. By focusing on positive, sustainable routines such as regular physical activity, a nutritious diet, and daily structure, you can build a strong foundation for mental well-being. The process of habit formation takes time and patience, but with consistency, these new behaviors will become second nature. By tracking your progress and celebrating small wins, you'll gain confidence and momentum on your journey toward improved mental health.

Chapter 7: Cultivating Supportive Relationships

The Importance of Social Connections in Recovery

Human beings are inherently social creatures, and meaningful connections play a vital role in maintaining mental health. When you're struggling with depression, it's common to isolate yourself, which can deepen feelings of loneliness, sadness, and despair. Conversely, having a strong support system can act as a buffer against depression and provide a sense of comfort, validation, and hope.

Studies have shown that social support not only helps reduce the risk of depression but also speeds up recovery. Positive relationships offer emotional support, practical help, and a space to express your feelings without fear of judgment. Knowing that others care for and believe in you can make a world of difference when you're feeling overwhelmed.

However, not all relationships are beneficial. The quality of your social connections matters more than the quantity. It's important to cultivate relationships that are positive, uplifting, and mutually supportive. In this chapter, we'll explore how to build a healthy social network, recognize toxic relationships, and ask for help when you need it.

How to Build a Positive Social Network

Building a positive social network involves surrounding yourself with people who uplift and encourage you. A positive social network can include friends, family, colleagues, support groups, or even online communities where you feel understood and supported. The key is to nurture relationships that are based on trust, empathy, and respect.

1. Start Small and Build Gradually:

If you've been isolated for a while, re-engaging socially can feel daunting. Start by reaching out to one or two people who you trust and feel comfortable with. Share small updates about your life and ask how they're doing. Over time, you can expand your social circle by joining groups or activities that interest you.

2. Be Intentional About Your Interactions:

Choose to spend time with people who have a positive impact on your well-being. These are people who listen, empathize, and make you feel good about yourself. Limit time spent with individuals who drain your energy or contribute to feelings of negativity.

3. Engage in Shared Activities:

Shared experiences strengthen social bonds. Look for opportunities to connect through activities that you enjoy, whether it's joining a book club, attending community events, volunteering, or taking a class. These shared activities can provide a natural way to build connections and form new friendships.

4. Be Authentic:

Building strong relationships requires being your true self. Letting others see your vulnerabilities fosters trust and deepens connections. It's okay to share your struggles and ask for support when needed. True friends will appreciate your honesty and will be there for you through both good and difficult times.

Recognizing and Addressing Toxic Relationships

Not all relationships are supportive. Some can be toxic, draining your energy and negatively impacting your mental health. Toxic relationships often involve manipulation, constant criticism, or lack of respect for boundaries. It's crucial to identify these relationships and take steps to protect yourself.

1. **Signs of a Toxic Relationship:**
   - **Constant Negativity:** If someone always focuses on the negative, criticizes you, or makes you feel worse about yourself, the relationship is not healthy.
   - **Manipulation:** If the person tries to control your actions, emotions, or thoughts, they are using manipulation to maintain power over you.

☐ **Lack of Support:** In a healthy relationship, support is mutual. If the person never reciprocates support and expects you to be there only for their needs, it's a sign of imbalance.

☐ **Disrespect of Boundaries:** If someone frequently crosses your boundaries or dismisses your needs, it shows a lack of respect for you as an individual.

2. Setting Boundaries:

☐ Boundaries are essential for protecting your emotional health. If someone's behavior is causing you distress, be clear and assertive about what you will and will not tolerate. For example, if a friend frequently calls you late at night to vent, let them know that you need to prioritize your sleep and would prefer to talk during the day.

3. Distance or End the Relationship if Necessary:

☐ If a relationship is consistently causing harm, it may be necessary to create distance or end it altogether. This can be difficult, especially if the person is a long-time friend or family member. However, prioritizing your mental health and well-being is paramount.

4. Seek Support When Dealing with Toxic Relationships:

☐ Ending a toxic relationship can be emotionally challenging. Seek support from a trusted friend, therapist, or support group to help navigate the process.

How to Ask for Help When You Need It

One of the hardest parts of dealing with depression is reaching out for help. Many people hesitate to ask for support due to feelings of shame, fear of burdening others, or believing that they should handle their problems on their own. However, reaching out is a sign of strength and a crucial step toward recovery.

1. **Identify Who You Can Turn To:**
   ☐ Make a list of people you trust—whether they are family members, friends, or professionals like a therapist. Think about who has been supportive in the past or who has shown concern for your well-being.

2. **Be Honest About Your Needs:**
   ☐ When reaching out, be as clear as possible about what you need. It can be as simple as saying, "I've been struggling lately, and I need someone to talk

to." Being specific helps the other person understand how to support you.

3. **Choose the Right Time and Setting:**
   - ☐ Choose a time and place where you can have a private and uninterrupted conversation. This makes it easier for both you and the other person to communicate openly.

4. **Accept Their Response:**
   - ☐ Not everyone may be equipped to offer the help you need, and that's okay. If someone is unable to support you, it's not a reflection of your worth. Continue reaching out until you find someone who can offer the support you need.

Exercises: Identifying and Strengthening Your Support System

Exercise 1: Identifying Your Support Network

1. Take a blank piece of paper and draw a circle in the center. Write your name in the circle.
2. Around this circle, draw other circles and write the names of people who are currently part of your support

network. This might include family, friends, mentors, or professionals.

3. Use different colors to indicate the type of support they provide (e.g., emotional support, practical help, etc.).

4. Reflect on the quality of these relationships. Are there people you want to strengthen your connection with? Are there any relationships that feel draining or one-sided?

Exercise 2: Reaching Out for Support

1. Choose one person from your support network whom you trust.

2. Write down what you'd like to share with them—whether it's an update on how you're feeling, a request for advice, or just a desire to spend time together.

3. Reach out with a message or a call. Be honest and let them know that you value their support.

Exercise 3: Setting Boundaries with Toxic Relationships

1. Identify one relationship that feels draining or negative.

2. Write down specific boundaries you want to establish (e.g., limiting contact, avoiding certain topics, etc.).

3. Practice how you will communicate these boundaries in a calm and assertive manner.

4. If you struggle to implement these boundaries, seek support from a trusted friend or therapist.

Conclusion

Social connections are a critical part of recovering from depression. Building a positive support network and maintaining healthy relationships can provide the emotional stability and encouragement needed to overcome challenges. By setting boundaries, distancing yourself from toxic relationships, and reaching out for help, you can cultivate a network that supports your mental health and well-being. Take the time to nurture these relationships and don't be afraid to seek the support you deserve, no one should have to face depression alone.

Chapter 8: Staying Motivated Through Setbacks

Understanding That Setbacks are Part of Recovery

Recovery from depression is rarely a straight path. It's a journey with highs and lows, progress and setbacks. There will be days when you feel hopeful and motivated, and others when you feel like you're back at square one. Experiencing setbacks doesn't mean that you've failed or that your progress has been erased, it's simply a part of the process.

Setbacks can happen for many reasons: a stressful life event, a change in routine, or even just an unexpected wave of emotions. When they occur, it's crucial to remind yourself that setbacks are normal and don't define your entire journey. The way you respond to these challenges is what ultimately shapes your progress. By learning to view setbacks as temporary and focusing on how to regain momentum, you can build resilience and continue moving forward.

Why Setbacks Happen:
1. **External Triggers:** Stressful events, relationship conflicts, work pressures, or physical illness can contribute to a temporary return of depressive symptoms.

2. **Internal Factors:** Negative thinking patterns, rumination, or a lack of self-care can also lead to setbacks.

3. **Expecting Perfection:** Sometimes setbacks happen because we set unrealistic expectations for ourselves. It's important to remember that progress doesn't require perfection.

The key is to approach setbacks with self-compassion and curiosity. Instead of blaming yourself or feeling defeated, ask yourself: *What might have contributed to this setback? What can I learn from it? How can I take care of myself during this time?* This shift in mindset can turn setbacks into opportunities for growth and deeper self-understanding.

Strategies for Staying Positive When Faced with Challenges

1. **Reframe Your Thoughts:**
   When setbacks occur, it's common to fall into negative thinking patterns such as "I'll never get better" or "All my efforts have been wasted." Challenge these thoughts by reframing them. For example:

- Instead of: **"I'm back to where I started."**

- Reframe to: **"I'm experiencing a temporary setback, but I've made progress before, and I can do it again."**

Positive self-talk can help reduce the impact of setbacks and keep you focused on the bigger picture.

2. **Create a "Resilience Plan":**

Having a plan in place for when setbacks occur can help you navigate tough times more effectively. A resilience plan might include:

- ☐ **Coping Strategies:** Make a list of activities that help you feel calm and grounded, such as going for a walk, listening to music, or practicing mindfulness.
- ☐ **Support Network:** Identify a few trusted people you can reach out to for support.
- ☐ **Affirmations:** Write down a few affirmations or reminders, such as, "This feeling is temporary," or "I am stronger than I realize."

3. **Reconnect with Your "Why":**

During challenging times, it's helpful to remind yourself why you started this journey in the first place. Revisit your goals, values, and the reasons you want to recover. Creating a visual reminder, like a vision board or a list of your "whys," can help reignite your motivation.

4. **Break It Down:**

Setbacks often feel overwhelming because we try to tackle too much at once. Instead, break your goals into smaller, more manageable steps. Focus on taking one small action each day, such as going outside for a few minutes or completing a simple task.

5. **Use Setbacks as Learning Opportunities:**
Ask yourself: **What triggered this setback? What were the warning signs?** By identifying patterns, you can create strategies to prevent similar situations in the future.

The Role of Self-Compassion and Patience

Self-compassion is one of the most powerful tools in overcoming setbacks. It involves treating yourself with the same kindness, concern, and understanding that you would offer a close friend who is struggling. When setbacks happen, the natural response is often self-criticism or frustration. But berating yourself only deepens feelings of despair and shame. Instead, practice being gentle and patient with yourself.

1. **Talk to Yourself Like a Friend:**

If a friend came to you feeling discouraged about a setback, how would you respond? Likely, you would offer words of encouragement and remind them of their strengths. Try speaking to yourself in the same compassionate tone.

2. **Embrace Imperfection:**

Recovery is not about being perfect; it's about making progress. Understand that healing takes time, and setbacks don't erase the work you've already put in.

3. **Practice Self-Soothing Techniques:**

Self-compassion can be practiced through small acts of self-care, like taking a warm bath, enjoying a cup of tea, or writing yourself a letter of encouragement.

4. **Acknowledge Your Efforts:**

Rather than focusing solely on the setback, take a moment to acknowledge the efforts you've made so far. Give yourself credit for the progress you've achieved, no matter how small it may seem.

Celebrating Small Wins Along the Journey

One of the best ways to stay motivated is to celebrate your successes, no matter how small. Every step you take in the right direction is a win. Small victories, like getting out of bed, completing a task, or engaging in self-care, deserve recognition because they signify forward movement.

1. **Create a "Victory Journal":**
Each day, write down one thing you accomplished or a positive experience, even if it feels minor. This practice shifts your focus from what's going wrong to what's going well, helping you maintain a positive mindset.

2. **Reward Yourself:**
Give yourself small rewards when you reach milestones, whether it's enjoying a favorite treat, watching a movie, or taking time to do something you love. Rewards reinforce positive behavior and keep you motivated.

3. **Share Your Wins:**
Tell a friend or loved one about your accomplishments. Sharing your progress can deepen your sense of achievement and provide additional encouragement.

4. **Reflect on Your Growth:**
Periodically take time to reflect on how far you've come. Compare where you are now to where you were a few

weeks or months ago. Acknowledge the growth, resilience, and strength you've developed along the way.

Exercises: Setting Realistic Goals and Tracking Your Progress

Exercise 1: Setting Realistic Goals

1. **Identify Your Main Goal:** Write down a goal that is meaningful to you. Make sure it is **Specific, Measurable, Achievable, Relevant, and Time-bound (SMART).**

2. **Break It Down:** Divide the goal into smaller, manageable steps. For example, if your goal is to "exercise regularly," a smaller step might be "walk for 10 minutes three times a week."

3. **Create a Timeline:** Set a timeline for each step. Keep it flexible and realistic to avoid feeling overwhelmed.

4. **Celebrate Each Milestone:** Mark off each step as you complete it and celebrate your progress along the way.

Exercise 2: Building a Resilience Plan

1. **List Your Coping Strategies:** Write down 5-10 activities that help you feel calm, centered, or positive.

2. **Identify Support Contacts:** Write down the names of 2-3 people you can reach out to during difficult times.

3. **Create Personal Affirmations:** Write 3-5 positive affirmations to remind yourself of your strength and resilience.

4. **Review and Use Your Plan Regularly:** Keep your resilience plan handy and refer to it whenever you encounter a setback.

Exercise 3: Daily Gratitude and Wins

1. **Start a Daily Log:** Each evening, write down:
   - One thing you're grateful for.
   - One win or achievement from the day.
   - One thing you're looking forward to tomorrow.

2. **Review Regularly:** At the end of each week, look back at your entries to see how far you've come. This practice can help you maintain perspective and stay motivated.

Conclusion

Setbacks are a natural part of the recovery journey, but they don't have to derail your progress. By cultivating self-compassion, staying positive, and celebrating small wins, you can navigate setbacks with resilience and determination. Remember, every step forward, no matter how small, brings you closer to your goals. Stay patient, keep going, and know that your journey is a testament to your strength and perseverance.

Chapter 9: Sustaining Positive Thinking for the Long-Term

Maintaining Momentum After Recovery

Recovery from depression is a significant achievement, but maintaining positive thinking and emotional well-being over the long term requires ongoing effort and intention. Once you reach a point where symptoms have lessened or no longer dominate your life, the focus shifts from immediate recovery to maintaining and strengthening your mental health. Think of this phase as building a foundation that supports long-term stability and growth.

Maintaining momentum involves consistently practicing the techniques and strategies that helped during the initial stages of recovery—such as positive thinking, mindfulness, and healthy habits—while also being mindful of new challenges or stressors. Staying proactive and regularly checking in with yourself can prevent relapse and keep you on a positive trajectory.

The key to sustaining positive thinking is to integrate it into your daily routine, making it a natural part of your mindset rather than a forced effort. Over time, these practices will become second nature, enabling you to navigate life's ups and downs with resilience and a positive outlook.

Tips for Maintaining Momentum:

1. **Establish a Daily Practice:**
Continue incorporating positive thinking exercises into your day, such as affirmations, gratitude journaling, or setting daily intentions. Even spending a few minutes each morning reflecting on what you're grateful for or what you want to achieve that day can set a positive tone.

2. **Stay Connected to Your Support Network:**
Keep nurturing your relationships and seek support when needed. Even during good times, maintaining your social connections helps reinforce positive emotions and provides a safety net for when challenges arise.

3. **Monitor Your Thoughts and Emotions:**
Regularly check in with yourself. Are negative thought patterns creeping back in? Are you feeling overwhelmed or disengaged? Catching these early signs allows you to address them before they become major issues.

4. **Be Open to Adaptation:**
As you grow and change, your needs may evolve too. Be flexible and open to adjusting your strategies. What worked during the initial stages of recovery may need to be refined or replaced as you enter new life stages.

5. **Celebrate Your Progress:**
Take time to acknowledge how far you've come. Celebrating milestones, no matter how small, reinforces positive behavior and keeps you motivated.

Developing Resilience for Future Challenges

Resilience is the ability to bounce back from adversity, adapt to changes, and continue moving forward despite setbacks. While maintaining positive thinking can keep you grounded, building resilience equips you to handle future stressors and challenges without losing your emotional balance.

1. Strengthening Your Mental Flexibility:
Resilience involves being mentally flexible—being able to shift your perspective and adapt your approach when faced with new situations. This mindset allows you to see

challenges not as insurmountable obstacles but as opportunities for growth and learning.

2. **Cultivating a Growth Mindset:**
Embrace the belief that you can learn, grow, and become stronger through challenges. Instead of viewing difficulties as threats, see them as chances to build new skills and gain insights.

3. **Practice Emotional Regulation:**
Develop strategies for managing difficult emotions, such as deep breathing, meditation, or visualization. Being able to regulate your emotions during stressful times prevents overwhelm and helps you respond with clarity and intention.

4. **Create a Personal Resilience Toolkit:**
Compile a list of resources and strategies that help you cope with stress, such as favorite self-care activities, calming techniques, or inspirational books and quotes. Having these tools readily available can make it easier to regain balance during tough times.

The Importance of Continued Self-Care

Self-care is not a luxury—it's a necessity for long-term mental health. While self-care often gets more attention during recovery, it's just as crucial after reaching a stable point. Continued self-care prevents burnout, enhances emotional resilience, and supports overall well-being.

1. **Make Self-Care a Priority, Not an Afterthought:**
Integrate self-care into your daily schedule, even when you're busy. This could include physical activities like exercise, mental activities like reading or learning, and emotional activities like connecting with loved ones or engaging in hobbies.

2. **Balance Work, Rest, and Play:**
A healthy lifestyle includes time for productivity, rest, and enjoyment. Balance your responsibilities with relaxation and fun. This balance is key to preventing stress and maintaining a positive outlook.

3. **Listen to Your Body and Mind:**
Pay attention to signs of fatigue, burnout, or stress. Practice self-compassion by adjusting your routine as

needed, taking breaks, and allowing yourself to rest without guilt.

4. **Continually Explore New Avenues of Joy and Relaxation:**

Keep experimenting with new activities or experiences that bring joy and relaxation. Whether it's trying a new sport, learning an instrument, or spending time in nature, finding new sources of joy keeps life enriching and meaningful.

Finding Purpose and Joy in Everyday Life

Purpose is a key element in sustaining positive mental health. Having a sense of purpose gives life meaning and direction, motivating you to keep moving forward even when challenges arise. While purpose can come from big achievements or career goals, it can also be found in small, everyday actions and connections.

1. **Identify What Gives Your Life Meaning:**

Reflect on what brings you joy, fulfillment, and a sense of contribution. Is it helping others, pursuing a passion, creating something new, or simply spending quality time with loved ones? Understanding your personal sources of purpose will guide your decisions and actions.

2. Incorporate Purpose into Daily Life:

You don't have to wait for a big achievement to feel purposeful. Find ways to incorporate small acts of purpose into your daily routine, such as volunteering, expressing gratitude, or working toward a personal goal.

3. Focus on Experiences, Not Just Achievements:

Purpose isn't only about what you accomplish; it's also about how you experience life. Cultivate mindfulness and be fully present in the moment, appreciating the simple joys in life, like a beautiful sunset, a good conversation, or a creative project.

4. Stay Open to Growth and Exploration:

As you evolve, your sense of purpose may shift. Stay curious and open to new experiences that can expand your horizons and deepen your understanding of what brings you fulfillment.

Exercises: Long-term Goal Setting and Reflection

Exercise 1: Creating a Long-Term Vision

1. Envision Your Ideal Future:

Take some quiet time to visualize your ideal life 5-10 years from now. Imagine what you're doing, how you feel, and what kind of person you have become.

2. Set Three Long-Term Goals:
Based on your vision, write down three long-term goals that align with the person you want to become. For example, one goal could be related to your career, another to personal growth, and a third to relationships or hobbies.

3. Break Down Each Goal:
Outline the steps needed to achieve each goal. Include short-term and medium-term actions that will lead to your larger vision.

4. Review Regularly:
Check in on your goals every few months. Are you on track? Do you need to make adjustments? This practice will help you stay aligned with your long-term vision.

Exercise 2: Building a Daily Positive Thinking Routine

1. Morning Affirmations:
Each morning, write down three positive affirmations that reflect your goals and values. For example, "I am resilient and capable of handling any challenge."

2. Evening Gratitude:

Before bed, list three things you're grateful for that day. This practice helps reinforce a positive mindset and keeps your focus on the good in life.

3. **Weekly Reflection:**

Set aside time once a week to reflect on your thoughts, emotions, and progress. Ask yourself:
   - What went well this week?
   - What challenged me?
   - What am I proud of?
   - What's one thing I can improve?

Exercise 3: Finding Joy in Everyday Life

1. **Create a Joy List:**

Write down 10 simple things that bring you joy, such as walking in nature, listening to music, cooking, or connecting with a friend.

2. **Integrate One Joyful Activity into Each Day:**

Choose one item from your list to incorporate into your daily routine. This could be as simple as savoring a cup of coffee in the morning or taking a few minutes to enjoy a sunset.

3. **Share Your Joy:**

Engage in activities that not only bring you joy but also involve others, like sharing a meal or surprising a friend with a kind gesture. Shared joy deepens relationships and enhances well-being.

Conclusion

Sustaining positive thinking over the long term is about more than just preventing relapse; it's about thriving. By maintaining momentum, building resilience, practicing continued self-care, and finding purpose and joy in everyday life, you can create a life that feels balanced, meaningful, and fulfilling. Remember, this journey is ongoing, and every day offers new opportunities for growth and positivity. Keep embracing the process, and know that your continued efforts are paving the way for a brighter and more resilient future.

Chapter 10: Personal Stories of Overcoming Depression

Stories of others who have faced depression and found their way to healing can be a powerful source of inspiration. This chapter features real-life accounts of individuals who used positive thinking and mental resilience to overcome the darkness of depression and regain control of their lives. Each story is a testament to the strength of the human spirit and the power of shifting one's mindset, even in the midst of despair.

As you read these stories, remember that everyone's journey is unique. The paths shared here are not meant to be a one-size-fits-all solution, but rather, they serve as reminders that recovery is possible and that change begins with the courage to take the first step. Whether you relate to these experiences or find new ideas to apply to your own situation, let them be a beacon of hope and encouragement as you continue on your own journey to healing.

Story 1: Sarah's Journey Finding Light in the Midst of Darkness

Sarah had always been an optimistic and driven person, excelling in her career and maintaining a busy social life. However, after a series of personal setbacks—a painful breakup, the loss of a close friend, and overwhelming work pressures—she found herself sinking into a deep depression. Sarah felt lost and alone, questioning her worth and struggling to find any reason to get out of bed.

One day, a friend introduced her to the idea of positive thinking and suggested she try a gratitude journal. Skeptical at first, Sarah decided to give it a try, writing down just one thing she was grateful for each day. The entries started small: "I'm grateful for my morning coffee," "I'm thankful for my dog's wagging tail." But as the days passed, her list began to grow, and she started to notice a subtle shift in her mindset.

Realizing the power of this small practice, Sarah expanded her positive thinking exercises. She began setting daily intentions and challenging her negative thoughts by reframing them. When she caught herself thinking, **"I'm worthless and will never be happy again,"** she would consciously counter with, **"I am worthy of love and joy. I am taking small steps to rebuild my happiness."** It wasn't easy—some days, the negative thoughts were louder than others. But slowly, Sarah began to regain a sense of hope.

Today, Sarah continues to use positive thinking techniques as part of her self-care routine. While she acknowledges that the journey wasn't linear and that she still faces challenging days, she now feels empowered to handle them. Her story is a reminder that even in the midst of despair, small changes can create a ripple effect, leading to profound transformation.

Takeaway: Positive thinking may feel forced or insincere at first, but it's a muscle that grows stronger with practice. Start small, and allow yourself to build from there. Over time, those small shifts can add up to big changes.

Story 2: James' Story Overcoming the Trap of Perfectionism

James had battled depression for most of his adult life, but it wasn't until he started therapy that he realized the role perfectionism played in his struggles. Every time he fell short of his high expectations, he spiraled into self-criticism and hopelessness. He was trapped in an endless cycle of setting impossible standards and berating himself when he couldn't meet them.

His therapist introduced him to cognitive behavioral therapy (CBT) and the concept of challenging automatic negative thoughts. Initially, James found it difficult to believe that changing his thinking patterns could make a difference. However, after practicing the technique of "thought stopping" and replacing harsh self-judgments with more compassionate language, he noticed a shift.

For example, when he caught himself thinking, "**I'm a failure because I didn't finish my project on time,**" he would pause and reframe: "**It's okay to need more time. My worth is not defined by my productivity.**" At first, it felt unnatural, but as he continued the practice, he found that his emotional reactions to setbacks became less intense.

James also started using visualization techniques to help reframe his experiences. When a challenging situation arose, he would close his eyes and imagine himself as a supportive friend, offering words of encouragement and understanding. This visualization exercise helped him cultivate self-compassion, breaking the cycle of perfectionism and self-criticism.

Takeaway: Perfectionism is a common trap that fuels depression, but it can be overcome by challenging negative thoughts and learning to offer yourself the same kindness you would extend to others.

Story 3: Maria's Path Finding Purpose Through Positive Action

After being diagnosed with depression in her mid-30s, Maria felt trapped in a cloud of sadness and purposelessness. She struggled to find motivation and couldn't see a future where she would feel fulfilled. Her therapist suggested she focus on finding small ways to create meaning in her daily life.

Maria decided to start volunteering at a local animal shelter. Initially, she took on the role reluctantly, unsure if it would make a difference. But as the weeks went by, she noticed that the act of caring for the animals walking them, feeding them, and simply being present brought her a sense of peace and purpose she hadn't felt in years.

Seeing the positive impact of this small act, Maria expanded her positive actions to other areas of her life. She began reaching out to friends she hadn't spoken to in a while, offering support and lending an ear. By focusing on what she could give rather than what she was lacking, Maria's mindset began to shift. She realized that even in her darkest moments, she still had the power to contribute and create joy for herself and others.

Today, Maria describes her depression as something that still "knocks on the door occasionally," but she feels better equipped to handle it. She knows that by taking positive action, even when it feels hard, she can create small moments of purpose that build up to a meaningful life.

Takeaway: Purpose doesn't have to come from big achievements; it can be found in small, everyday actions. Focus on what you can contribute, and let those small acts of meaning guide you out of the darkness.

Lessons Learned and Takeaways from Real-Life Examples

These stories share a common theme: recovery from depression involves small, intentional shifts in mindset and behavior. While there is no one "right" way to overcome depression, these stories highlight several strategies that can be applied to your own journey:

1. **Start Small and Build Momentum:**

Each story began with small, manageable changes—whether it was practicing gratitude, reframing thoughts, or volunteering. Don't feel pressured to transform everything at once. Choose one small step, and focus on consistency.

2. **Challenge Negative Thoughts:**

Depression is often fueled by distorted thinking patterns. Learning to recognize and challenge these thoughts can reduce their power. Practice questioning negative thoughts and replacing them with more balanced, compassionate ones.

3. **Find Purpose in the Everyday:**

Purpose doesn't have to be grand. It can be found in small acts of kindness, moments of connection, or personal growth. Focus on finding small ways to create meaning in your daily life.

4. **Embrace Setbacks as Part of the Process:**
Each person faced setbacks, but they learned to view them as part of the recovery journey rather than as failures. Be patient with yourself, and remember that progress is not linear.

Encouragement for the Reader to Start Their Own Journey

If these stories resonate with you, know that you're not alone. Each of these individuals started where you are—feeling lost, overwhelmed, and uncertain of the path ahead. But through small changes and the courage to keep going, they found their way to a brighter place. You have that same strength within you.

You don't need to have it all figured out to start. Begin with a single step: try a gratitude exercise, reach out to a friend, or write down one positive affirmation. Each small step builds upon the last, creating a pathway to healing. Let these stories inspire you to take your own journey, and remember your progress no matter how slow matters.

You have the power to rewrite your story, one thought, one action, and one day at a time. Keep going. Your brighter days are ahead.

Conclusion

This book has taken you through a journey of understanding depression and exploring the transformative power of positive thinking. By addressing the root causes of negative thought patterns and providing strategies to cultivate a healthier mindset, each chapter aimed to equip you with tools to navigate the complexities of depression and build a brighter, more resilient life. Let's recap the key takeaways:

Key Takeaways from the Book

1. **Understanding Depression:** Recognize that depression is not simply sadness; it is a complex condition with physical, emotional, and cognitive components. It's important to approach it with compassion and seek support when needed.

2. **The Power of Thoughts:** Your thoughts have a profound impact on your emotions and behaviors.

Learning to identify and shift negative thinking patterns is a foundational step in overcoming depression.

3. **Challenging Negative Thoughts:** Techniques such as thought-stopping, reframing, and cognitive restructuring can help break the cycle of automatic negative thoughts and replace them with more balanced, supportive perspectives.

4. **Building a Positive Mindset:** Positive thinking is a skill that can be cultivated through practices like affirmations, gratitude, and focusing on strengths. It's not about ignoring difficulties but learning to approach them with a constructive mindset.

5. **Managing Stress and Anxiety:** Depression often coexists with stress and anxiety. Mindfulness, breathing exercises, and setting healthy boundaries are essential for maintaining mental balance.

6. **Creating Healthy Habits:** Positive routines, regular exercise, and good nutrition significantly impact mental health. Implementing small, sustainable habits can gradually transform your overall well-being.

7. **Cultivating Supportive Relationships:** Meaningful connections are vital in the healing process. Build a

network of supportive individuals and learn to communicate openly about your needs.

8. **Staying Motivated Through Setbacks:** Setbacks are a normal part of recovery. Practice self-compassion, celebrate small victories, and stay committed to your long-term goals, even when progress seems slow.

9. **Sustaining Positive Thinking for the Long-Term:** Recovery is an ongoing journey. Maintaining momentum, building resilience, and integrating self-care into your life will help you stay positive and cope with future challenges.

10. **Personal Stories of Overcoming Depression:** The experiences shared in this book highlight that you are not alone. Recovery is possible, and there is hope, even in the darkest times.

Encouragement to Continue Practicing Positive Thinking

Positive thinking is not a one-time solution but a lifelong practice. Just like building physical strength through regular exercise, developing mental resilience and positivity requires consistency and dedication. There will be days when maintaining a positive outlook feels difficult or even impossible—but these are the moments when it is most crucial to persist.

Start small and be gentle with yourself. Integrate positive habits into your daily routine, such as starting each morning with a gratitude exercise or ending the day with a few positive affirmations. When setbacks occur, view them as opportunities to strengthen your resilience rather than as failures. Remember that each effort you make, no matter how small, contributes to your overall growth and healing.

A Final Message of Hope for Readers Facing Depression

If you're reading this book, you've already taken a brave step toward healing. Facing depression is not a sign of weakness but of strength—the strength to acknowledge pain, seek understanding, and strive for a better life. The journey through depression can be overwhelming, but it's important to remember that you are not defined by your struggles. There is hope, and there is a path forward, even when it seems invisible.

Recovery may not be a straight line, and it's okay to move at your own pace. Allow yourself the space to feel, to grow, and to stumble along the way. Healing is not about eliminating every negative thought or emotion, but about building a life that feels meaningful and manageable, even with the challenges that arise.

You have the power to change your story, one thought and one action at a time. Let the tools and strategies in this book be your guide, but know that your journey is uniquely yours. Embrace the process, celebrate your courage, and keep believing in your capacity to overcome. With time, patience, and perseverance, you will find the light within yourself that depression has tried to dim.

You are stronger than you know, and you are worthy of joy, peace, and fulfillment. Keep moving forward, one positive thought at a time. Your brighter days are ahead.

Appendices

The appendices provide additional resources and tools to help you on your journey to overcoming depression and maintaining positive thinking. Whether you're looking for further reading, professional support, or practical worksheets to reinforce what you've learned, this section is designed to complement the strategies discussed throughout the book. Take advantage of these resources to continue building resilience, understanding your mental health, and practicing positive thinking in your daily life.

Appendix A: Resources for Further Reading

1. **Books on Cognitive Behavioral Therapy (CBT) and Positive Thinking:**
   - **Feeling Good: The New Mood Therapy** by Dr. David D. Burns
   A comprehensive guide to CBT techniques for overcoming depression and anxiety.
   - **The Happiness Trap: How to Stop Struggling and Start Living** by Dr. Russ Harris
   An insightful book on Acceptance and Commitment Therapy (ACT) and how to build a meaningful life.

- **The Power of Positive Thinking** by Dr. Norman Vincent Peale

A classic guide on using positive thinking to achieve emotional and spiritual fulfillment.

- **Self-Compassion: The Proven Power of Being Kind to Yourself** by Dr. Kristin Neff

Focuses on the importance of self-compassion and offers practical strategies to build it.

2. **Online Resources and Websites:**

- **Psychology Today**: www.psychologytoday.com

A directory of mental health professionals, articles, and resources.

- **Mind**: www.mind.org.uk

Provides information on mental health, including depression, self-care, and seeking support.

- **National Institute of Mental Health (NIMH):** www.nimh.nih.gov

Offers research-based information on mental disorders and treatment options.

3. **Videos and Podcasts:**

- **The Happiness Lab with Dr. Laurie Santos**

A podcast that explores the science of well-being and practical strategies to build a happier life.

- **TED Talks: The Power of Vulnerability** by Brené Brown

A powerful talk on embracing vulnerability and building emotional resilience.

4. **Workbooks and Journals:**

- **The CBT Workbook for Mental Health** by Stephanie Fitzgerald

An interactive workbook with exercises and tools for managing depression and anxiety.

- **The Gratitude Journal for Mental Health**

A structured journal to practice daily gratitude and foster positive thinking.

Appendix B: Mental Health Support and Helpline Contacts

If you or someone you know is struggling with depression, anxiety, or other mental health challenges, don't hesitate to seek professional help. Below is a list of mental health support and helpline contacts that can provide assistance, resources, and guidance.

United States:

- **National Suicide Prevention Lifeline:** 1-800-273-TALK (1-800-273-8255)
- **Crisis Text Line:** Text "HELLO" to 741741
- **Substance Abuse and Mental Health Services Administration (SAMHSA):** 1-800-662-HELP (1-800-662-4357)

United Kingdom:
- **Samaritans:** 116 123 (available 24/7)
- **Mind Infoline:** 0300 123 3393
- **Shout:** Text "SHOUT" to 85258

Canada:
- **Crisis Services Canada:** 1-833-456-4566
- **Kids Help Phone:** 1-800-668-6868 or Text "CONNECT" to 686868

Australia:
- **Lifeline Australia:** 13 11 14
- **Beyond Blue:** 1300 22 4636

International Helplines:
Visit www.befrienders.org for a global directory of mental health support helplines.

If you are in immediate danger, please contact your local emergency services.

Appendix C: Worksheets for Thought Tracking, Goal Setting, and Positive Thinking

Use the following worksheets to reinforce the strategies discussed in the book. Each worksheet is designed to help you identify negative thoughts, set meaningful goals, and maintain a positive mindset. Feel free to photocopy or print these worksheets to use on a regular basis.

1. Thought Tracking Worksheet

Date	Situation	Negative Thought	Emotions Felt	Alternative Thought	Outcome

Instructions: Use this worksheet to track negative thoughts as they arise. Write down the situation that triggered the thought, the thought itself, and the emotions you felt. Then, practice reframing by writing an alternative, more positive thought. Finally, note the outcome and how this exercise influenced your mood.

2. **Goal Setting Worksheet**

Goal	Why is this Goal Important?	Steps to Achieve it	Potential Challenges	Support Needed	Deadline

Instructions: Identify a specific, measurable goal that you want to achieve. Outline why it's important to you and the steps you need to take. Consider potential challenges and the support you might need. Set a realistic deadline to keep yourself accountable.

3. **Positive Affirmations and Gratitude Journal**

Date	Positive Affirmation For Today	Three Things I am Grateful for

Instructions: Begin each day by writing down a positive affirmation that resonates with you. Then, list three things you are grateful for. This exercise will help you start the day on a positive note and build a habit of gratitude.

4. **Self-Care Plan Worksheet**

Area of life	Self-Care Activities	Frequency	Notes

Physical Health	E.g., Exercise, Nutrition	Daily/Weekly	
Emotional well-being	E.g., Journaling, Therapy	Weekly	
Social Connections	E.g., Phone a Friend, join a group	Weekly/Monthly	
Spirituality	E.g., Meditation, Nature Walks	Daily	

Instructions: Fill in the areas of life where you want to focus on self-care. Identify specific activities that nurture your well-being, and note how often you plan to engage in each one. Use this plan as a guide to ensure you're prioritizing self-care in your daily routine.

These worksheets are designed to be flexible and adaptable. Feel free to modify them as needed to fit your personal goals and preferences. By regularly practicing these exercises, you'll continue building the skills and habits necessary to maintain positive thinking and support your long-term mental health.

With these resources at your disposal, I hope this book serves as a valuable companion on your journey to overcoming depression. Remember, the road to healing is not always linear, but every step forward is a victory. Keep using the tools and strategies provided, seek support when needed, and believe in your capacity to create lasting positive change.

www.ingramcontent.com/pod-product-compliance
Lightning Source LLC
Chambersburg PA
CBHW050804250726
48653CB00006B/2073